THANH DINH

The Smallest God Who Ever Lived

First published by Writerly Books 2025

Copyright © 2025 by Thanh Dinh

All rights reserved. No part of this publication may be reproduced, stored or transmitted in any form or by any means, electronic, mechanical, photocopying, recording, scanning, or otherwise without written permission from the publisher. It is illegal to copy this book, post it to a website, or distribute it by any other means without permission.

Thanh Dinh asserts the moral right to be identified as the author of this work.

Thanh Dinh has no responsibility for the persistence or accuracy of URLs for external or third-party Internet Websites referred to in this publication and does not guarantee that any content on such Websites is, or will remain, accurate or appropriate.

First edition

ISBN: 9781069499806

This book was professionally typeset on Reedsy. Find out more at reedsy.com

For all the lost souls: Blessed are the suffering that made the human in us

Contents

1	The Smallest God Who Ever Lived	1
2	Acknowledgement	2
3	My Mother	3
4	I Almost Believe It	5
5	A Phone Call from Japan	7
6	Thou Shalt Not Kill	9
7	What Happens After Death?	10
8	The Dark Side of the Moon	12
9	Burn	15
10	Nietzsche Said	18
11	Reading Virginia Woolf	20
12	By Nightfall	22
13	Not Even Laughter	23
14	The Death in the Garbage Truck – Prelude	25
15	Living is About Killing Everything	27
16	The Death in the Garbage Truck – Interlude	30
17	The World is Onto Me	31
18	The Death in the Garbage Truck – Epilogue	33
19	Bones	35
20	Screaming I'm Sorry to the Mirror	38
21	That's It, Just Let Yourself Go!	41
22	Keigo	44
23	What You Call Freedom	48
24	It Gets Darker	51

25	My Therapist	53
26	Skin	56
27	The Promise – Prelude	59
28	As I Lay Sleeping	60
29	Touch	62
30	About Giving Up	64
31	Truth Be Told	66
32	Don't Try	68
33	The Promise – Epilogue	70
34	Hiraeth	71
35	He falls first. She is destroyed by choice.	74
About the Author		85
Also by Thanh Dinh		87

1

The Smallest God Who Ever Lived

First Edition
By: Thanh P Dinh (she/her)

2

Acknowledgement

I will not be able to compose these poems without the help of my family, who is always there for me, in the darkest of times as well as in the brightest of times. Thank you, Ma, for tolerating the craziness when the night creeps in. Thank you, Sister, for helping me choose the best works to include in this collection, as well as for proofreading the whole book. Thank you, Pa, for never losing hope in me, as well as my work.

I want to offer my thanks to two other people outside my family – my professor, Dr. Richard Greene of the University of Toronto Mississauga, who never doubts my talent and always does his best to guide me on the literary journey, and my muse, K., who has forgotten me but will always hold a special place in my heart.

The works in this collection are my sole creation. I do hope they will help the readers as much as they helped me in recovering myself. After all, to quote Lynn Crosbie's words, "Life is about losing everything."

3

My Mother

I don't talk enough about my mother – no one does
    I don't talk enough about the late-night thoughts
    Running in the wilderness of her mind
Like a sandstorm passing through
While I am lying by her side, spasming
Convulsing,
Gasping for air
And for the living.
I don't talk enough about the tears
Dropping, dropping, dropping
Down her sunken cheeks
Lined with wrinkles and worries and sorrows
Enough for a whole lifetime, and somehow,
She will still have enough left over
For the next lifetime,
And the ones after that.
I don't talk about the youth she had,
The one where she had to be abandoned to learn to love me;
The one where she had to beg for food

So that I can live in the luxury
Of depression and the pile of antidepressants lying on my nightstand,
Blooming like a beautiful flower, and by so doing,
Ends its life;
Nor did I talk about her parents: my unknown grandparents –
The ones she thinks about often
When she gazes out of the barred windows of the large, empty kitchen,
Singing, "Mother don't you know,
life is always filled with sorrow
and you are nowhere to be found,"
I don't talk enough about my mother, and by that, I mean
that I just let her suffering tears
rain down the desert of my heart, hoping that
one of these days, the flowers will grow
and I can prove to my therapist
that I, too, can learn to be human again.

4

I Almost Believe It

You stand there, hidden behind the screen
　　of unforgettable memories and the unseen future,
　　and wonder, How to break her
in the cruelest way, in the tenderest phrase,
And still makes her chase
After shadows and phantoms and the aftermath
Of the burning forest of 'what could have been'
After life, and after you?
And you tell her, "I always think about the truth,
And the truth has always been that I loved you."
You forget that she knows about the past,
And while you are moving back and forth on your scheme,
Lying through your teeth, hoping that you'd seem –
What's the word? Faithful.
But she is faithless. Broken in the heart, and broken in the head,
　　Broken in the chest, and broken in the skeleton,
　　Broken at the core, and broken on the shore
　　Of the promises you never think about enough

THE SMALLEST GOD WHO EVER LIVED

To keep in your heart, now and forever more.
So when you said that you would love her again,
I just laugh until my heart falls out of my mouth
And sadness drops down from my lips –
You know when you lie like that,
I almost believe that you mean every word –
The word in the future, and the word in the past,
The word in the goings, and it is going fast.
After so many deceits, you'd think I'd known better,
But still, I almost believe it.

5

A Phone Call from Japan

First published on Wishbone Word Magazine

I wake up to the sound of your voice – the tremulous tone,
The broken English, and the heavy stone
Of longing for something more
Than whatever my human heart can give.
I wake up to the laborious pronunciation of your laugh –
The night is cold, the snow frost hardens the windows of my apartment,
The winter slithers into my blanket and I can feel
The noose of your suffering reaching its hand out
To squeeze the remnant of life through my hoarse throat.
The pain is suffocating enough that I can feel the word 'Save me'
Runs through my veins to reach my vocal cord,
And comes out of my lips as, 'I love you.'
I plunge right through the immense field of snowflakes,
Trying to find the image of the you I had bet all my life to forget,

THE SMALLEST GOD WHO EVER LIVED

Hoping, believing, deifying
A being that is bleeding from the heart
And bleeding everywhere.
I know it isn't fair, but who would take the chance to share
The responsibilities of shooting rockets to the sky,
Thinking it would reach the moon?
Until when would the field of the snowflakes end,
Bringing with it the remaining of your image,
And the life that you've lost?
Oh honey, I don't think living would cost any more than that,
And with thousands of miles in between,
I still wish upon that phone call from Japan
That you'd be living again.

6

Thou Shalt Not Kill

Moses said, Thou shalt not kill.
    Judging from the endless wars that were, are, and will be
Burning down the forests between you and me,
I guess that Moses' words,
Like the religions that were, are, and will be
The excuses for dying with the death,
Had fallen on deaf ears of his disciples.
"But Moses," they said, "We must have a war to end all wars,
And in wars we kill, we maim, we destroy
Whatever that is not to our advantages and our joys."
And much like Moses' words,
His disciples' greed
Falls deaf on him, too.

7

What Happens After Death?

First published on Wishbone Word Magazine

I hold Death in my arms like an old lover –
His skin and bones hang around me,
And hang around everywhere.
He tells me about the places he has been,
The wars he waged, the battles he lost,
And the lives he took
In sweet revenge of the human who shook
After hearing his name.
"You are right, honey, you are right," I say,
"But what happens after that?"
He stays silent, mad with the fever for living with the living,
And sad with the longing for dying with the death.
He says, "Nothing happens after it –
Perhaps we all disappear, and perhaps we all live through the mist
   Of forgetfulness and regret.
Remember the soldier's life in the year of 1975
When he wrote his last words on a blood-dried note:

WHAT HAPPENS AFTER DEATH?

'I lay down my life to make you free,
And dearest mother, do not forget about me'?"
I tell him that the story belongs to a period of old:
A period of longing for the tender hold
Of a loving soul, whose name history will thank
But will never write down on the page of the forsaken,
And the forgotten.
"But darling, remember, remember, remember –"
And all I can say to him was,
"Never, never, never."
It is fun when you negate Death:
He's always fidgeting about the dying
And the ones we forget.
How can one live after loving him, and how can one leave the safe net
Of a vast nothingness and an immense abyss?
"You must always know me before you start loving me," he said when we first met.
"I know you," I said, "All that's left to do
Is to understand you,
And the life you took – will continue to take."
Not the perfect first date, I know,
But he agreed, for the forgotten ones' sake.

8

The Dark Side of the Moon

Sitting in this empty place where some call home
 Some call 'the Earth'
 And some only call it a fleeting dream, a fickle
Theatrical stage play
 Where the actors and actresses are bursting for life at the seams
 And try their best to make the costume fit,
 I remember the story about the first dog that went into space.
 I don't know her name, and perhaps on another sleepless night,
 When the wind whispers so closely to my ears
 And the tears are always on the verge of
 Falling, falling, falling
 On my eyes,
 I hope I can understand her sorrow and solitude
 And recall in the multitude of waves washing back to the shore
 I will recall her name once more.
 I heard on the news that the dog never made it to space alive.

THE DARK SIDE OF THE MOON

Some pragmatic people will prefer that fact over my truth;
The truth that she is still living,
Breathing in the stars
And eating out of the craters on the moon.
The truth is that she is living on the dark side of the moon,
Barely missing the people who betrayed her last look of despair
And her longing to go home, soon.
The truth is that she only wants to live
But the livings always have their own sacrifices;
And in this temple some call Earth,
Some call anguish,
Some call madness,
She was chosen out of hundreds and thousands of beings,
Like a scythe in the night, swiping her head off,
And leaving the entrails everywhere,
All of that to prove that there is nothing on this planet
That humans cannot destroy.
With truths like that, I'd prefer believing that she is alive,
Somewhere out there, waiting for the call home.
Isolated, alienated, shattered, and broken into tiny pieces of the undead,
She is waiting for the call for help.
Perhaps that is the reason all Gods choose to leave(
After all, we are no longer the humanity
That He'd consider allowing a second chance
At living through the fast lane and chasing through the rat race
Only to be invited to a place more superficial
Than this Earth.
Perhaps paradise is the idea of the herd;

And despite His wanting, or not wanting,
Paradise is still there, construes from the bones and flesh and blood
Of a thousand lives on Earth.
He shows no mercy, and He forgives no shepherd;
And yet we still wonder why He does not love us –
The children who built Him an empire
Only to watch it fall
Into the shape of a teardrop on the statue of Mary full of Grace.
I don't know this place. I'm living on the dark side of the moon,
And it is pretty good here, where all you can see is the darkness of the dying stars,
The bursting of life in an abyss of nothingness.
Yet some still doubt if there was life on Mars.
Not I, I say to the disbelievers,
I will wait for the dog, and the rocket will take us home,
And on the dark side of the moon,
There is imprinted the solitude
Of a race chasing after happiness
Only to dissolve into madness too soon –
See, sitting here at this place some call Faith,
And others call Faithless,
No wonder I never find anything less than
Solitude,
And a tinge of bitter sadness.
How does one survive after love,
And after Death?

9

Burn

I remember telling you about Joan of Arc -
    about how she sacrifices herself to the flame of Paris
    and how her white bridal dress turns into shards of glass
piercing through my veins as I look into your eyes
through the lenses of blurred memories.
I remember reading through your words to weave myself
a world of dreams - full of deceit and lies and non-existent promises
but a beautiful world nonetheless.
I confess
I never consider waking up in the morning an option
until you come and tell me that I can live the life of a butterfly -
continue dreaming and forgetting the rest
because of all the things that happened to me, you are the beautiful mess
that I never knew I needed but always knew I wanted.
I guess
all I want to say is I want the pain -

the pain of being burned in the Hell you create -
the Hell of the vainly selfless and the selfishly hopeless.
Your lies are eternally burned into my skin like the fever of a child
in the sultry winter of the dark, cold Winterland.
I hold onto the agony and the pain, thinking, This is life -
This is living.
I reach out both of my hands toward the stake, begging -
my eyes were blinded by the Christmas lights and the peppermint candies -
through the frosted windows, I can see a happiness that is so close to me
like a snowflake, and when it touches my fingertip,
I can feel it melting into my being and into nothingness.
My lips quiver but I can't feel my tears -
They are falling, falling, falling
like the first snowflakes of spring.
No one knows they are there, but sometimes, people are reminded of their existence
in a cold wind.
I remember telling you about Joan of Arc -
but does it ever matter?
I guess what I wanted to say was
if you wanted to build a fire,
to brighten the window light,
to warm the love that you never have for everything that's living
and everything that's dying,
then I would be the first one to jump into the flame.
Your lies burn me, and if you see me now -
my skin is blotched with scars that lead to the palpitating

heart
  that has always been beating for you.

10

Nietzsche Said

Nietzsche said that God is dead,
    And that we were the ones who had killed him.
    I don't know what hurts me more:
That God is no longer walking on water
To reach the shore,
Or that since the beginning yonder, over the hill
Of life and of what would become after life,
I have never once in my existence
Believed in Him.
I guess it seems superficial – the atheist in her sorrows
Decides to believe in miracles
And the being that science cannot prove into being
And into surviving
The wars of attrition, and of being the victors
And the vanquished.
You see, sadness is not a feeling:
It is there on the waves, washing off to the shore;
It is the wind whispering,
'You are here no more,"

NIETZSCHE SAID

Not caring that you are trying to be less than happy,
And less than suffering for Heaven's sake.
Nietzsche said, God is dead
And we were the ones who had killed him.
The stream of God's blood turns water into wine,
And turns wine into something akin to
Almost happiness.
Thank you, Nietzsche. Thank you for being a believer
Of emptiness and the voiceless abyss
That still echo in the darkness that is shrouding
The windows of the skyscrapers,
Shapeless and soulless,
As soon as the evening slips off her evening dress
And bury the human beings in her bosom
Of loneliness.
Thank you also
For believe that humans are strong enough
To kill a being that never was
And always is.

11

Reading Virginia Woolf

Reading Virginia Woolf
  One can finally find oneself
  Immersed in the rolling of the words
And the dancing of the lines,
Curving, swaying, laughing,
And doing anything to make oneself
Feel the burning of life again.
After all, Virginia Woolf never wants to make it darker
Neither does she want to make it less than anything
But all the future that she sees and seems,
Sparkling inside her heart like a beacon of lightning and thunder
And the silence of shapeless dreams.
Reading Virginia Woolf
One finally finds within oneself
The reason to fight again,
To try again,
To live, not for oneself, but for living's sake,
To drown in the lake of solitude, wandering,

READING VIRGINIA WOOLF

And the night is creeping up from the bottomless ocean
Like an old lover that one refuses to mention in one's memory
And in the intimacy of one's tears, dropping
In the dark, with the fear of being discovered
That one does not know how to love
Just to live again.
The resurrection of something more than a bargain
For the sinless and the sinned –
The resurrection of believers of the same Gods
But different religions –
The resurrection of something more than the selfless and the self –
And one can say to oneself,
I am alive again.
Reading Virginia Woolf,
One must wonder
With all that genius,
Life, from the beginning, was never hers to hold,
And to understand her,
One has to let things go at that.

12

By Nightfall

By nightfall, I had already succeeded in killing half of myself. I don't know where the other half is; perhaps it was never there and never will be: it is free to roam the night as it pleases. It starts haunting the sorrow of the past and the suffering of the future. It is everything that I want to become and everything that I never want to face. Slowly, I track down the other half of me in the shrouding darkness. The starless sky descends to Earth and in the bottomless ocean, they become one whole again, making eternity seem like something only the senseless understand. Someone demands immortality as the right of the living and the free; but hasn't he already realized? None of us is free, and none of us escapes the shackles of being and nothingness. By night fall, I had already succeeded in killing a half of myself, and if God is true – if He is real – I will manage to kill the other half comes the morning, when the air is still, and the breath is suspended in between the hanging of the heart and the seal of the Pandora box, beating for the things that I will never become. Then, and only then, will I believe in something as fickle and joyless as immortality.

13

Not Even Laughter

He didn't leave you much, did he -
    after all the miseries He endured, I doubt that
    He would use miracles to cure humans
of sadness.
I can feel the chaos of an ocean of pain -
desperate and loveless -
drip, drip, drip
onto my eyelids.
And do you think it fits for Him
to bring down anything else but wrath, anger, and a slim chance
  of being the victor. See outside your windows: the conquered
  and the victor walk side by side -
  their limbs are made of paper-thin wire -
  and they ask for not much, not even laughter. The choir
  sings the hymn of His love, but yonder -
  petrified and crucified -
  He just laughs. You'd think He never has a heart to begin with
-

but the last shred of red cloth has been torn and shed
on the last human when He disappeared -
because nothingness must return to nothingness; did you hear
the hymn rises in your ear, up, up, up -
until it becomes the raindrops - and for years upon years,
it will drip, drip, drip - look at the tears you shed -
it consists of oceans of suffering,
of the help that He is bestowing, loveless and cold,
of the hands reaching out to hold on,
and the hands letting go.
We are not made of gold,
and no human is born strong enough to withhold
the blows dealt him by a God who, in his holiness,
favors cruel souls.
He didn't leave you very much, did He? Show me
a smile,
a laugh,
a happiness – untainted
the last salvation you still possess -
I will ask for nothing less -
since the day I became Godless,
I have always been free, but the shackles tightened around my ankles
tell me He'd always be there
to catch the rebels like the day the Babel Tower fell.
I can hear thunder, and as the ocean drips, drips, drips,
I close my eyes and weep for the things that never were,
and the things that never will be.
Yes, He didn't leave you much, not even laughter.

14

The Death in the Garbage Truck – Prelude

"Well, what d'ya wanta know? He's done time with life. Now he's down there doing time with death," the man chews the bamboo stick, "Either way, a poor bastard lived a poor bastard's life and died a poor bastard's way." And she asks, "What happened before that? Was he - was he depressed? Was it suicide? What did the company say?" And the old, decrepit man says, "What the Hell's 'depressed'?" He squints his eyes against the glare of the sunlight, "An' why woulda sonabitch choose death when he can choose to live on?" And she says, "I don't know. Perhaps he's just - just too sad to live." The old man laughs, "You fuckin' stupid bourgeoisies with your fuckin' stupid bourgeoisie idears. "Too sad to live," eh? And what can death do about it? The only thing it can do is to bring more sadness. Listen here, missum, have you seen his wife and mother?" And she says, "I haven't had the chance, and nobody tells me their address. I hear that they move somewhere far away." The old man snuffs his cigarette, "Then you haven't seen pain yet." All is silent. The old man chews the butt of the cigarette. Does he think about Death, then? Or does he think about the soullessness and the nothingness of the life he led up until now? Why did the sonabitch choose to tear his life in half? The old man didn't know then and certainly does not know now. But given the choice all over again, he'd still choose to live – the show must go on, and the now will become a past no one wants to remember. Yes yes yes, he thinks to himself, It's all the fault of these bourgeoisie. After all, who'd die from sadness?

15

Living is About Killing Everything

The scientist says that once every seven years,
The living cells kill each other and appear as emperors in new clothes:
Naked and cold and struck to the core – much like how gold
Must go through fire to be something people want –
Something akin to a shining – dreaming, hoping, vanquishing
Everything that is us
And nothing that will become of us after the show's ending.
The scientists always find joy
In killing everything – and by believing in them,
I find reasons to kill anything that is a part of me – the memories
The miseries, and the eternal suffering
That the non-existing religion was trying to keep me burning, screaming,
"I have no choice left – I only want to be living."
How cheap is the word "alive"?
The labeling of humans as something that always will be an ending

And will never be a means to anything else but
Something that's rotting and dying at the core
And dying in between.
Every morning, I wake up, repeating to myself,
Be alive, be alive, be alive,
And try not to only survive – let's make a bet against life,
Let's tell life that we are all existing,
Doing our best not to kill everything,
Because after all, to repeat another day like this,
We must imagine to ourselves that we are happy.
The ever-after we long for is not Cinderella – rather,
We prefer to be anything else other than us – than human, all too human.
Life is about killing everything,
And as you are reading this,
A living cell is bestowed on a dying cell
By killing it softly, tenderly, sweetly,
Like the lullaby that your mother sings to you as you are sleeping,
Dreaming of a world
Where beasts and children can also believe in something as fickle as being happy.
Yes, living is about killing everything,
And the next time I go to my therapist, I will stick an honorable badge on my lapel.
"What can I do, my dearest therapist," I will say,
"After all, I survived. I've been surviving all these years."
I hope that after reading this poem, pondering, and wondering
About what could have been me instead of what's living in me,

He will put me on a new antidepressant.

16

The Death in the Garbage Truck – Interlude

"Listen, missum," the old man sits down by her side and pats her trembling shoulders, "I am no God or philosopher, but I think it is because we are all raised to be strong, to be so God damned strong." And she says, "But I am not strong." And the old man laughs, "That's the cause, the man laughs, No one is built to be that strong. And whoever built this world keeps demanding, More, More, More. And we keep on begging, Don't ask for too much of us. Neither comes out as the winner. And that's the war. That's the God damned war." He looked intently into her eyes, only to receive a questioning glance, "But what if we win?" And he says, "Missum, if we had the chance to win, the sonabitch would have been alive." And that seems to be the answer to all existential problems: If we had the chance to win, the sonabitch would have been alive.

17

The World is Onto Me

The leaves of the old oak tree in front of the blinding balcony,
    And sea foams are bubbling up only
To die down, again, again, and again,
And they whisper to me, It's not dark yet.
Of course, everyone knows it's not dark yet – but
How can one know what will happen after that?
The leaves of the old oak tree snicker,
The laughter in the dark,
The holler of the devastated beggar,
And the lovers, it is always about the lovers –
As billions and billions of years further down the path of the suffers,
    Adam and Eve were, are, and will forever be
Banished for the crime that created the first human to walk on the surface of the Earth.
    Of course, if you do not believe in God,
    That is just another lie to lessen the pain your soul feels, the heart

Aching for something that would last longer
Than a promise.
The leaves of the old oak tree whisper, It's not dark yet,
And Atlas has not shrugged his shoulders – the boulder on his back
Keeps falling down the abyss
And keeps dying, screaming, shouting into the nothingness
Of its own existence: Let us all be a-burning
Let us all be the living.
Your throat constricting, you are choking
On the very words that would save you
From the wrecking plan of a God that is too high and mighty
For you to be released from being
And from barely surviving.
The leaves are whispering, Just let it go,
But how can one let go of one's own shadow
And one's own existence?
You refuse to believe in anything other than the benevolence
Of the One that you had forgiven, the One that was forsaken
Before all else had taken shapes and forms
To create in you the Him that will always be living,
Immortalized by the greed and the illusion
Of a race that does not know anything better
Than to kill and to maim
The leaves of the old oak tree whisper, You just have to believe,
But you know better than to jump down the edge of dreams,
And the edge of faith – after all, you know the trade,
And the world is onto you,
And the world is onto me.

18

The Death in the Garbage Truck – Epilogue

The old man sees her to the cab, closes the door, and waves her away like any other journalist who has been coming and going to this God-forsaken town for many months. She clutches her bag to her breasts and watches the red brick buildings float by. The starving eyes of the hungry children follow her to the doorstep of her company. Their dark, bottomless irises stand starkly against the murky yellow background that should have been their whites. If she closes her eyes long enough, she can feel the eyes carve away her flesh slowly until they reach the heart and gouge it out for the children to eat. Perhaps this is what N. feels, she thinks, and how can one live like that?

She closes her eyes in the cool air-coned room. The document opens on her computer screen, but there are no words. She dreams of the garbage truck, of the old man sweeping the trash from the stuck sewer, and of N. And there inside the turbine of the truck is her corpse, torn apart, lifeless. The old man and N. keep on sweeping and stuffing trash onto the garbage truck.

Life moves on, and she is happy at last. *That is the cause*, the old man says to N., *No one is built to be that strong.* And the garbage truck drives into the darkness.

19

Bones

I dig up eight feet of dirt and instead of sticks and stones
I hit the jackpot of bones.
I read somewhere that the _____ Canal of the great USSR was built on corpses
and though I find it hard to believe at times, I must reconcile with the human in me
to acquiesce that humanity is always capable of being cruel.
The universe out there is quiet at night, and on some nights, you can hear the moon howl
with desperation and loneliness and cold.
Two hundred fifty thousand miles away and I wonder what she wants from the old Earth.
Look at our history: there's nothing but wars.
We made wars against wars and wars against peace,
and even the Ares must agree that He raised his children so brilliantly that once the wars end,
the winning sides always kill themselves.
I hold the bones to my bosom and hear them crack under the pressure of the living

and freedom.

Here are my forefathers, lying bare in the mass grave somebody dug for the purpose of distinguishing

between the slaves and the masters,

the enemies of the people and the rulers,

the counter-revolutionaries and the true ideologists.

You past beside their names a nice label, and suddenly, the rotting bones of a thousand people

do not sound so bad.

After all, it's just human killing other humans, and aren't you glad you are not a part of that?

I hold the bones, and they turn into dust; on them carved the words, Not yet.

I can foresee the future where my children, my grandchildren, and many others

will come here to the mass grave called Earth, holding my bones, asking themselves,

What is the story she would like to tell

if she had had the chance to live longer, to fight harder, to exist, to suffer?

But they don't need my memoir for that: their bones are carved with the stories

many before them had gone through,

and many after them will keep on repeating.

I point out to them the bones of the villagers at My Lai,

the bones of the soldiers defending Gac Ma Island,

The years were 1968 and 1988, but they don't need to remember the time:

their life had not yet begun while others had turned to dust and I don't blame them for that.

I just want them to hold onto the bones, see the carvings, see

BONES

the crying,
 the last words of the soldiers dying
 defending the piece of land on which they are standing.
 The stories need not be repeated because it is muddied with blood and gunshots;
 the rifles will keep on shooting.
 Somebody shouts, You must kill to be the living
 because to stand still is the job of the dying,
 and who would want to be among the dying?
 They always say it is not immoral to choose life.
 But the bones say differently: We all come here to stay,
 and it may not be immoral to choose life
 but it is a different matter to feed your life on another's.
 Perhaps all the bones need is none other than to be free.
 And if my next generation asks me about my country's family tree,
 I won't need a textbook, a history course, empty words and phrases
 and analyses on analyses;
 I will tell them, Look for your bones, and look at them intently,
 listen to their silent cry and see them shine their beauty
 on a lonely moonlit night.
 Look for the bones of Gac Ma, of My Lai,
 and there you will see the whole course of our forefathers' struggles and their fight.
 It may take two hundred and fifty thousand miles to go to the moon,
 but all you need to do is travel back in time,
 to find your home and to kindle the flame in your soul,
 are the bones.

20

Screaming I'm Sorry to the Mirror

Just to hear the apology echoes back and reverberates around the bathroom
    In the form of a feeble "I love you,"
Knowing that love never was strong enough to cure anything
Besides the disillusionment of a being
Who refuses to be a being – you'd think
That she would know better than believing in a dream – the prelude
Of death
And the epilogue of a life
She never had – but no,
She'd rather have faith
Because believing is always better than
Barely living.
Apparently, religion is the end-all
For the faithless and the weak, but after all,
No human beings are built that strong.
She knows this, and she screams to the mirror,
I am sorry,

SCREAMING I'M SORRY TO THE MIRROR

Like a vestige of the last thread of hope,
Hanging from the edge of existence
Of something that is akin to love.
I want to tear off the mask you wear
And the fake laugh that tells others how much you want to be in their life –
How can I tell you, repeatedly, until the nights can make you
Fall in love with silence again, that you are fine – like how the aged wine
That is continually pouring into your champagne glass
Which people call happiness, and which you call,
Your perfect solitude.
How can you, of all people, treat me like an object
With pity in your eyes and mockery on the tip of your tongue – another figment
Of your imaginary sadness?
And I am always afraid that one of these days,
You will fall down, down, down
Until the only thing that remains of you
Is my memory of the day your wrist cuts itself
On something that will make you a human again.
I am always afraid that one of these days,
I will lose you to something
Other than an apology, whisper thinly in the closed air of the bathroom –
Do I love you, I wonder, And do I hate me enough to let you win?
Both questions I cannot think through
But you always know enough to pull both of us
Out of this mess.
And until the day you know more than enough to not whisper

an apology to me,
   I will whisper into your ears
   The honey nectar of sweet-nothing loves.

21

That's It, Just Let Yourself Go!

That's it, just let yourself go!
    Because you know not what lies in the show
    That some call life,
And others just call it "passing by."
You neither know what costume you'd wear
When you reappear on the stage again – but you know
That the saints will not take you in their hands
And embrace you in the love that the Bible promises
When you first picked it up, hoping, dreaming, believing
Against all odds – and all evens
That you would be living again, resurrecting from the fruitless ground
    The very earth that built you up, only to strike you down
    Again and again and again
    As if it were your duty ever since the ruin of Rome
    To be maimed and broken.
    No, give your thanks to the storm that you pray for so fervently
    Just in case one of these days,

It will be your first hope and your last salvation – ere the storm's second coming
You fear you'd be dying with the living
And living with the dead.
No, give your hatred towards the force that keeps you be
Instead of the force that allows you not to be – ere before that force's second coming
You were nowhere to be found
Except within me.
No, don't give your thanks to the fellows passing you by,
Saying you have much more to love than life itself,
Because what is life, if not the chance to cause chaos and mayhem
And if one of these days you were given the chance to do it all over again,
The mayhem will still be there, remaining
As the last source of hope – the worst demon out of Pandora's box –
As the last source of whatever you need
To keep on existing.
What is life? You asked yourself this question
A thousand times and again, repeating
The riddle that none of the living can solve
And all the dead had died trying to unfold
As if by merely repeating it, you, too,
Would be able to add another day to the current day,
To connect the past to the present
And the present to the future.
You realized you don't dread living – you are simply scared
Of holding on.
So that's it, just let yourself go.

THAT'S IT, JUST LET YOURSELF GO!

And perhaps the one of these days you so often dream of
Will fall down, down, down,
Descending from the shoulders of Atlas
Into the embrace of your bosom,
Hoping, by so doing,
It had saved you from the world.

22

Keigo

I heard you changed your job again.
 I thought I had known you better than to believe in the nonsense you make
about promises and the oath to be by each other's side despite the earthquake
 that is sweeping across the land, and darling, the Babel Tower
 had long fallen down, so if you come to me in full armor and ask me
 "What are you talking about?"
 I would still understand.
 I heard you needed me -
 just like you need another piece on your chess board to win against life.
 I think I would cry but who knows that you have long pushed me past the point of pity.
 I ask you if you have read Shakespeare
 and if you have known about Hamlet,
 and you tell me you are ready to listen to everything I say
 as long as I pay for it.

Thus I don't have the chance to tell you about Ophelia,
about how she goes crazy after Hamlet kills her father
and her love for him is so strong that it pushes her over the lake
and she dies in the coldness of winter.
But of course, I am not Ophelia.
You always tell me that I am stronger than you are.
Darling, it would take much more than strength and courage alone
to send a message in a foreign language across the ocean
hoping that the person who receives it will find hidden among the nonsense
something akin to love.
I burn the scarf I knitted for you just to watch the last sparkles of your voice
die out on my skin
and carve out the map of Japan.
Amidst the pain and the silent cry, I can point out on my skin
the shape of Tokyo and your smile.
"You are so kind," you often say, "so why,
why would you ever need me?"
You put so much contempt in kindness as if to point out to me
that kindness does not feed the poor and certainly,
it does not make money grow on trees.
Darling, of course, I see how my kindness kills me.
In the sleepless nights, I can feel kindness tower over me like the final Titan that Zeus cannot kill
and even Atlas cannot bear its weight; so he shrugs and the Earth crumbles to pieces.
I pick up whatever is left of my kindness and crush it in the

palm of my hand
   just to feel the beating of Life's heart.
   Isn't it wonderful to know that Life still has a heart,
   and that it will burst under the touch of a feather?
   You know, I'd rather be Ophelia.
   Only in darkness can you see the spark of kindness grow.
   Perhaps Ophelia saw it, and like the moth be to the flame,
   she sank deeper into the lake, hoping that kindness would warm
   her corpse.
   In that way, one can imagine that in the last hour of flickering hope,
   Ophelia was happy.
   But again, this was just nonsense. A make-believe ending. A tower of promises
   that I lay down on the foundation of the fallen Babel Tower,
   hoping that in the spring or summer, when the last snowflake of winter
   melt away in the bosom of the lake where Ophelia lay,
   I can build a bridge across the ocean to reach Yokohama Bay.
   I heard you changed jobs again.
   I thought I had known better than to believe in anything that life has to offer.
   But even the Babel Tower falls and Atlas shrugs,
   so what else can prevent me from digging up the dirt with my bare hands
   only to scream your name into the void
   and bury the sound of my voice into the nothingness of Life's beginning?
   I roll each syllable of your name on the tip of my tongue
   and taste the frozen snowflakes of last winter.

KEIGO

The cherry blossoms bloom, and it will soon be summer,
but your name is forever here, carved deep in the tissues of my flesh
and on a silent night, you can hear my bones creak; in their breath,
I can hear them say, "That's it, just let yourself go."
And perhaps it would make you happy to know
that, like Ophelia, I jump into the frozen ocean,
hoping that on a nice summer weekend,
my bones will reach Yokohama Bay.

23

What You Call Freedom

Is what I call surviving
   Wars after wars after wars
   With myself.
I thought – had thought, and blessed be Thy Name, still think
That by surviving the darkness
I can finally find out what freedom means –
What it feels like in the burning palms, which
Are attached to my body like a useless tool, shouting, screaming,
Help me.
I can almost taste freedom on my tongue –
Did you know that freedom has the shape of a sad song –
The drug ballad,
The amphetamine eulogy,
The dopamine and serotonin that you had long forgotten –
Except when you are face-to-face with yourself in the bathroom,
Looking straight at the mirror,
Wonder, "How much hatred can one hold in one's own

pocket?"

Chewing repeatedly the nicotine, tasting the bitterness on the tip of your tongue

Thinking, I am at peace,

And I agree, you are at peace,

But you forget the question at the beginning of every argument,

Are you free?

Or are you just like me, caught and kept inside a box,

Thinking, dreaming, longing for another life,

Not mine, obviously, because who'd want to trade everything they have

To become the same person they were yesterday – the person They want to kill?

Do you still believe in faith – in religions?

In their ability to save you and build you a home

Out of broken dreams and the fragmentary illusion

That you can leave the house whenever you have the option –

The time bomb is ticking, saying, You are never escaping,

After all, religions are not to be handled

Like a painkiller – a fantasy, a rush of adrenaline to stop you from breathing

While the trees are whispering, Wake up,

You were never destined to be here, or there, or anywhere.

You are you, and I wish that could mean freedom,

But it only means death.

Walking ahead, I can only drag you along, lifeless,

Limbs hanging out of the oxcart

Like the body of a private, killed in battle,

Never surviving long enough to become a monument

Of your own existence.
And yet, you still think is this – whatever it is,
Is the very meaning of freedom – no, darling,
What you call freedom
Has always meant surviving.

24

It Gets Darker

If you want something light,
   You shouldn't pick up this book.
   If you want something encouraging –
Something happier, funnier, warmer – everything that is more
And is never less,
Then you absolutely shouldn't pick up this book.
You know, I thought hard about the hook of the song –
The happy-ever-after,
The fairytale ending, the home at the end of the world,
The dreams I chase, the homes I make,
And the me I leave behind
To follow the footsteps of others before me – to jump down the cliff
Screaming, I am living the life.
But I failed. I was not born with a golden voice –
I am more of a beggar, trying to will the choice to live.
No, I am happy – of course, what else can I be?
I've got everything I want – I get to breathe

While many others fall down at the broken place
Trying to face the scythe of Fate,
Hoping that, through the broken fissures,
The light will shine through,
And the light will save them –
And the light did shine through,
Reaching them where they hurt the most,
Piercing to the core of their existence,
Screaming into their ears, Who will save me?
Do you have pity
For the tireless lights – the ones who try and try and try,
And a thousand yesterdays
Combined with a million of tomorrows
Only to build this moment that we call today,
But the ones who try cannot reach the sky,
The Babel Tower done fallen down,
And the show must go on, of course,
Whether the lights shine through or not,
Whether the ones who try
Can make it
Or not.
We fall through the cracks of Heaven,
Not to reach Hell,
But to reach the Present – so no,
If you want the light,
You absolutely should not pick up this book.

25

My Therapist

My therapist says to me, "You don't have to forget to forgive"
    She is always full of fun lies like that
To get me through the strange earth, shattered
Under my every step – as if this earth is refusing me,
Dragging me,
Swallowing me
Into its own darkness,
And I don't want to admit to my therapist,
But sometimes it's sad to think that the Earth's success
Overwhelm all the angels' herald within me
And my will to live.
My therapist says, "You must love yourself
Before you learn to love others."
But she does not teach a girl of twenty-year-old
How to hold one of her hands in the other,
Telling her, "It's alright, I forgive you
For existing."
She does not teach that girl

That she sees every three months
How to survive without the strength of another person,
Lifting her up, up, up
Only to throw her down into the abyss,
Saying, "I only love you
Because you are the last innocent creature on this Earth."
How absurd,
She thought love could be bought with more than
A cruel sentence and a silhouette of almost a man.
My therapist says, "You must know that you are special."
But she does not say that when everyone is special,
No one is.
I tell my therapist, "I only want to be – to live and not feel guilty
That my existence is strangling the girl within me,
That I want that girl to be free from the monsters
I carried with me since the early age of sixteen and look,
I know that it's not any of my business, any more than it is hers,
But I know that girl can benefit from a little drop of the elixir
Called love.
I know you don't care for her existence – in fact, you'd call her a demon,
But she is the only thing I have left – the only thing
That almost means freedom."
My therapist says, "You should get out more,"
And before our session ends, she says, "You'll live."
As if I haven't been doing "the living" right,
As if this living thing is scored on a curve,
And the best I can get is a C-minus.
But I'm through with it.

MY THERAPIST

I toss the lies into the trash can,
And walk out of her office.

26

Skin

I look at my wrist with the thick patch of skin cutting across the white surface
    and it looks back at me, saying, Not yet.
I hide my razor in a place no one can see - my head
is full of dreams and miseries
running side by side like two racing horses -
sometimes one of them cuts ahead, but I never know which one it is -
which one will bring me more happiness and which one will bring peace.
I push ahead with the word 'anyways' and each step I take
cuts deeper into my skin than the scar on my wrist -
everyone tells me it's brave to hit life in the face and bear the slit throats
and the thick battered skulls -
but nobody ever tells me that life has no face, and more often than not,
you will end up with slit throats and battered skulls.
A famous writer once sulked,

SKIN

Those who life cannot break, it kills.
How could he expect me to believe him when life kills him, too?
I sometimes think about the monsoon moon
and the rain on the terrace of flooded rice paddies and the asphalt road
leading to a place with leaden clouds and soon,
I see myself digging up dirt to build a mausoleum for the life that I had shoved away -
they say she has gone astray;
you can only see the passing of her silvery ghost when the May rain falls
on tin roof, whispering in the summer leaves for all to hear:
I am abandoned, forsaken, a heedless sacrifice for the things that no longer borne
a will to live.
The moon looks at her and says that
it's fine to leave - wherever you arrive,
we will all be by your side. And I ask,
Who are "we"?
I live in the singular reality,
I look at the moon and say, There is only one of you and one of me.
I seize my hands and feel the life I already gave away seeping through the cracks -
I thought the armor I had was stronger than that.
And the thick patch of skin on my wrist stares back in the cold, silent night -
Not yet, not yet, not yet.
You know, they said
that God builds a special Hell and we call it Heaven on Earth

where each of us hides a razor blade in the brain and waits for the burst
of a call to arms,
of the piercing scream that penetrates the calm night,
of the rain that falls on a tin roof,
of the whisper in a conversation with monsoon moon -
and we don't need proof that we live a life:
we tie our shoes, pick up our razor blades, push ahead with an "anyways" -
They said, Not yet, but do you know what life says?
It says, Here we go again.

27

The Promise – Prelude

The lights of the stage were on, and there you were, standing on the stage in the white suit, turning your back to the audience. I can hear the protagonist's voice ringing, But I loved you. You lowered your head on the word "love," and I wondered how much solitude a shoulder can hold. You stepped away from the stage; I stood up, my lips quivered, my hands reached out, and my whole skeleton trembled. Don't go, I mouthed to the darkening stage, but it was too late. The whole audience stood up for a standing ovation, but you were no longer there. The only thing I have left until this day is a photo of you and me, and the ticket stubs from that day. How long has it been since the day you breathed life into me? And how much longer can I hold onto this agony, watching the back of your white suit fading into the darkening theater so the lights could go back on, and the audience will live, while in that little corner behind the curtain, I died again and again, a hundred times over.

28

As I Lay Sleeping

The bombs keep blasting in the police stations
and on the mountains, the people are beaten –
lifeless corpses are lying across fields and vacated
crossing –
  the phantoms of the past are screaming, Let our young go –
  and you can hear from the mountain ranges' hollow
  the howl of the lives laid down so their children can stand
proud -
  but the piece of land, but the commercial values
  of the money that the mountain people can never get
  and always left unused.
  Hush and listen to the lull of the willows
  When an old mother holds out her hand, saying
  "Save my child" - he was twenty-nine
  with a wife and children –
  they are waiting for the last man standing
  to come home.
  Under the grove, the grotto, the cave, the willows weep
  for the life that is shedding, prostrating on the altar of power

AS I LAY SLEEPING

look, a sacrifice made but no one knows for what
and the new settlers keep throwing stones
on the bodies whose owners know not for what to atone.
A wife covers her husband,
"May God of the Sun saves His humans" - she prays
to the invisible being that represents non-existence
and by the rushing streams, you can hear the sunspots weep -
while the new settlers flay the husband's body
in retribution for the policemen's corpses.
Who cares about the escaped reactionary –
the ideals no one believes but is always ready to kill to protect?
As I lay sleeping, the bombs kept blasting on the mountains,
the lives keep on losing,
The blood keeps on flowing into the river, onto the sea.
The whole Earth moves
and the mountain people are begging for the life that is rightfully theirs –
all of this happens, all of this, all of this,
as I lay sleeping.

29

Touch

Feverish fingers dance on porcelain skin,
    leaving behind them the touch of scorching passion –
    Bruising kisses –
Wet tongues on dry lips –
Someone forgot to tell Joan of Arc
She was dead –
The stake burns through the night
And the flesh comes ablaze –
Living has never been so bright in all its writhing malice –
And while she breathes through the misery,
The fingers stealthily slip through her leatherette strap –
Burn, burn, this agonizing thirst –
Where is the love that is rumored to cure all sufferings that could be?

And you can hear the quivering voice of her smoldering desire escape –

Through close lips, tongue-tied, her head turned, she whispered his name to the endless void

That once was her existence:

TOUCH

I thought you were mine –
Spelling out the pain, soft as feathers falling on skin –
Before the Earth moves,
the feverish fingers keep trailing on her skin,
Leaving behind a map of the wasteland –
The country every stranger wishes to visit
But none yearns to stay –
Leaving is just another trait of human nature –
And who is she to wage a war against the system?
Raindrops on spring leaves –
Like playing a sonata from centuries of old
the cold sound of the piano keys thumbing on the eardrums –

She watches the rain fall on the petals of the cherry blossom –

The snow melted, burying a part of her to the dream of him. Yet –
Something was born of darkness, and something
was born of truth.
Her lips whisper his name again when the winter thunderstorm strikes
and in her heart, carnage is the sovereign. How she wishes she could feign
Ignorance
and pretend to be Vices dressed in Innocence.
Feverish fingers. Blazing skin –
quivering lips, tongue-tied, silk dress slips through the cracks of the first dawn –
Remember that only in the aftermath of the quake,
You can feel the Earth move.

30

About Giving Up

She's a wolf.
When the moon strikes at midnight and its blue light paints a shadow of pain,
she turns into this hideous creature
moving along the shops' windowpanes:
her claws leave red blood on the pavements and her hair falls down the well;
is it her blood or someone else's?
And even if she knows the answer, will it make any difference?
She's a beast.
Her heart grows as big as the old fairy tales.
Perhaps when she was born, a witch left a curse on it.
A curse that looks like a red claw mark of the wolf looking at her:
His yellow eyes still haunt her dreams.
I will call you back, he said;
I will check the message you left, he said;
She doesn't know what to do when she hears words like that,
because the wolf always leaves in the end.

ABOUT GIVING UP

She's the moon.
Though there are hollow abysses and craters on her face,
she still manages to ride through the waves,
and when her beauty shines - once in a while - on the full moon night,
she brings the silver ocean to his lover, the shore:
She knows that now and forevermore,
there's no love for a moon that's a hundred thousand miles from it.
She's a girl.
Broken and destroyed and rusty - you name it.
She wasn't born this way; she promised you that,
but the rest is as old as time, and she never mentions it.
Of course, she knows lies when she hears them, she said,
but how can one give up on hope?
And when she asks you that, you will be stunned.
You don't know if she can distinguish truths from fiction,
or whether she sees through your facade.
You wonder what she wants: loyalty or another hurtful breakup.
Perhaps it will help your conscience when you know that
she's been long used to both.
I will call you back, you said,
And I will check my mailbox more often, you said.
She smiles through and through, I know.
She's a human.

31

Truth Be Told

that people believe more in sadness than in happiness -
it's an age-old knowledge and sadness
is contagious.
Sip a little from this cup of bitterness that we call life
and let's see if you can escape the whirlwind
of hopelessness and despair -
and why do you still love every bit of it?
Truth be told
that a long time ago
when God created Adam
He has prepared Himself for betrayal -
and why do you expect Him to love
when His love has long been exhausted?
Between cut-wrist and tongue-tied dead field of vast silence -

among the lamentations of the human
toiling over life and toiling to reach an end,
you can hear of His revenge.
Do you expect me to see Him as a God of Mercy, then?

TRUTH BE TOLD

Truth be told,
that He cares not for fame or glory -
among the battlefields and the wars of victory,
He walks among the lighted torch, the human corpses,
and the blazing fire of the winners,
His last words before rising to Heaven,
If your lifespan were that short,
why don't you spend it on something or than loving each other?
and what's use would it be, to what end?
Or do you just want a page in history dedicated to you
and the pains you caused
like how you petrified and crucified Me before?
Why do you always want more
and for as long as the tides come to meet the shore,
you always come to Me when nothing else works -
Do you believe in Me or in miracles -
fake and useless and dark as the Catacombs of Paris
built upon death, but nevertheless -
the miracles bring you happiness;
fleeting, yes, and disguises as white lies on the dark canvas
of desperation and an abyss of hopelessness.
He breathes the final exhausted breath
and disappears before the light reaches Earth -
you can see his haggard shadow imprinted in the mountains
and in your heart - have you noticed
how He sings in His loneliness?
Truth be told,
He was dead a long time ago.

32

Don't Try

Don't try –
    They will tear it down anyway –
    And by 'it' I mean whatever you are dreaming of building – think
Of Howard Roark and his ending –
The saying, "Well, at least he tried"
Becomes so bitterly hilarious you can almost choke on it laughing – think
Of Sisyphus pushing the stone up the slope only to watch it fall – think
Of Neil Armstrong looking at the Earth from outer space, realizing how lonely the human race is – think
Of Dostoyevsky's agony when he wrote, 'You were destined for me. Perhaps as a punishment.' See –
When you stop trying, living becomes unbearably light –
So light you can almost lift off the Earth –
But where's the fun in that?
Don't try. From the crushing wheels of cruel history
You have seen how trying has punished humanity – but oh,

darling
   The question keeps ringing and the devil keeps tempting:
   What if we fly?
   Don't try.
   And yet, trying is the only way for us to survive on this beautiful catastrophic stage
   Of the divine comedy
   We call living.

33

The Promise – Epilogue

I sit there watching the clock's hands move slowly by. It has been twenty-nine years. Exact to the date and the minute. No one ever guarantees that a promise is made to be kept. No one ever guarantees that you will come to this shop after all these years with a withered white peony bouquet only to compensate for the time you made my skeleton tremble under my skin. The Earth moved, and without knowing it, I let go of your hands for but a second only to lose you forever. But it's you we are talking about. You probably will say, It can't be helped because life is about losing everything. My eyes are wide open with tears. The stubs are on the table. The red wallet is torn at the corner. The photo grows blurry with time, and slowly, you are no longer in the frame.

"Ma'am, the shop is closing."

"I know. But I am still waiting," I say.

"For what?"

"A promise."

34

Hiraeth

I turn around, trying to find the place I belong to –
   The road leading to that foregone home
   Has long been buried in the snowstorms
Of the many winters I ignored
Because I grasped the greed of the living
Far too hastily –
I turn around, the sound of the empty promises reverberates in my ears –
   The sweetest song I will ever hear. The defeat is drawing near –
   And though that fact has been carved onto my body
   Like an ancient curse – a relic, forgotten, from the many centuries
   Of wars and peace – Yet the dying heart is still beating
   In my ribcage. How can one stop dreaming of the living
   And hoping for death? Outside, the cherry blossom is blooming –
   I can show you the fervent prayers – kneeling at the altar
   Of a God I never believe in, screaming in His deaf ears:

The Word is broken in between
And broken when you are here.
You see, I chase after the fleeting shadow of the hare
On the dark side of the moon.
My mind keeps saying, "Soon"
But my heart keeps begging me, "Never."
Where are you in this unfathomable ocean when it is baring the sharp white teeth
Ready to swallow the last shred of humanism? My feet
Walk on water, but you who are so in love with freedom and refuse to acquiesce
Should know that your wings can never bring you as far as
The life you are living in.
I whisper your name – each syllable sounds so foreign
That for a split second,
I forgot your face; the voice of many summers faraway
Dripping into my ears like the sweetest nectar of the first batch of honey –
I don't want you. I want all of you.
The droplets of desire burn my skin, and as the panic sinks in,
I run blindly ahead – what are we, if not the arch-nemesis
Of the right to be free?
You are my hiraeth. And I, your forsaken ghost – the unlived life,
The babe that breathes but only once before the weight of the world
Closes in.
Look at us running in circles. One has to admire the effort we spend
Just to burn each other at the stake of hatred.

HIRAETH

I don't hate you. I hate all of you.
I turn around, hoping that one day,
Stumbling in the snow of this foreign country
You will be there. Tell me a funny story.
Tell me how you can become my defeat –
The wounds on the head, the pulse in the palms,
The vanquished battle where I hold you in my arms –
Tell me how to unfold the misery we are living in
But don't tell me how to forget you again.

35

He falls first. She is destroyed by choice.

Kill My Darling – When Love Becomes Idolatry and Promises Are Gospel

Chapter 1: The Murder

February 14, 20XX

I chug down the sugary iced tea like there is no tomorrow. Maybe after tonight, there will be no tomorrow.

The disco ball is making my brain dance on its unsteady feet. My ears ring with the booming noise from the DJ floor. *Hi, my name is. Hi, my name is. Chicka-chicka-chicka.* I pull out a cigarette, light it up, inhale the delicious nicotine like my life depends on it. Fuck, I need air.

"Angela. Sweet Angela, hey, darling," a voice deafens what is left of my hearing ability. I turn to walk away but a strong hand stops me in my track, "Where's Bambi?"

"Fuck me if I know," I scowl.

"If I could, I would. But Bambi will kill me if I do, so I won't." Markus, the lecherous voice in the figure of a Greek God's appearance, leers. His hair combed back, polished and reeked with the smell of cheap money. The deep shade of brown makes me sick to my stomach. He sneaks one lanky arm around me, breathes in my ear, "Bambi owes me a few grands. For the last drug delivery, you know."

"I don't." I push him away, trying to repress the urge to vomit.

"Yes, you do, baby girl. He said if he's gone, I can talk to you." The sweet voice is now tinged with a hint of annoyance. He blabbers on and my stomach churns at the thought of seeing him dead.

"I seriously don't. And you've had your talk. Let me go." I hiss.

"Come on, angel. He's not –"

"Listen here, Markus." I turn on my heels, yank my arm away, grasp his collars, shove my face into his space until he can feel my raging breath and the sweet tea I just down, pissing these words into his ears, "I'm done with him. With you. And with anyone who's involved. Fuck Bambi. There's no him anymore. There's only me. You either get away from me or I swear there will be blood."

"Woah, sorry to ruffle your feather."

Markus watches in bewilderment as I stomp out of the crowded bar. I can hear his frustrated grumble as I leave the threshold, "What's wrong with that fucking bitch?"

Outside, the sky is lit up in a tacky red neon color. The air is filled with the sickeningly sweet smell of garbage and rotting waste. The flower district. The place for dreams to die. The same place to resurrect all kinds of passion available for human to purchase. I bite off the last bit of my cigarette, feeling the tears swelling up. Since when have I sunk so low? The fishnet legging revealing every bit of my skin, the crop top barely covers my breast, the piercings on my stomach, my lips, my nose, and my ears, the dark makeup, and the ocean blue hair.

I snort. 'There's only me' and what the fuck. Who am I kidding? I cut my wings because I believe in mortal sins. The sweet words of a human are far more tempting and worth believing than any gospel the blind religion can dictate. I'm no angel. I'm barely human. I choose to follow a god I can see and embrace with both hands, not the one I can't guarantee is there from the beginning. What I have left is a corpse with a beating heart. A zombie escaping an apocalypse, thinking it still possesses something like a will to power.

A wet feeling on my nostril draws me back to reality. I wipe my nose. It's sticky with a thin trickle of blood. I need my usual cocaine dose, but not now. My sanity is the last thing I want to lose. The craving is creeping on my skin. My hair stands on end. I shiver with the knowledge that somewhere in the glove compartment, Bambi hides his usual stash. Markus asked, "Where's Bambi?" I didn't feel anything then, but when the cold air hits my eyes and the stink in the car pervades my nose until I suffocate in a soft pool of sorrow, I finally feel the earth beneath me shatter.

I sit in front of the wheel, letting the silence comfort me, thinking to myself, "This will be the last time." Oh, Thou art my sweetest friend, my bitterest foe.

The cars speed by, racing down nowhere fast. I lean back on the driver's seat and put a playlist on. Bambi's raspy voice raps to the beat, "Just turn back and I will be here, waiting for you with cigarette smoke and coffee –." His lyrics are so agonizingly sweet and tender, filled with promises and ever-after that I have to laugh at the stupidity. But my tears have long dried and my heart burns with the little love I never knew I still possess.

Yes, fuck Bambi. The silver-streaked hair, slicked back, hard to the touch, the arrogant smirk bordering on contemptuous snicker, the wide grin when he's high on ecstasy, the beat ringing through the night in those drug parties as he spits out flow after flow, living on the edge of Hell and Heaven. What I would give to have it all back. What I wouldn't trade to never have known the sweet taste of his poison. I said, 'There's no him anymore.' What I meant was, 'There's only ever been him.'

I check the rear-view mirror. The blue neon light flickers in the dark, giving off an eerie feeling. The signboard says, *We can show you Heaven.* It's almost a cheap act of divine comedy how the people going there are looking for Hell instead. I inhale the sharp nicotine taste. Sweet Bambi. Cruel Bambi. Smart Bambi. Everything Bambi.

My youth has been wasted away in a chaotic whirlpool of madness and longing, reduced to the shape and sound of those five syllables name, Bambi.

I turn on the ignition and take a final glance at the bar, Rendezvous. So long, misery. I'm so glad I have other options besides dying with you in this whole mess. There are better things out there instead.

The glass gets foggy after a while with the heater on. The February night is piercingly cold. But I can't spend another moment breathing in the stinking smell of rotting flesh. I roll down the windows, stick my head out, and breathe in the dearly needed fresh air. The cozy restaurants along the upper side of the Lakeshore Boulevard are filled to the brim with couples enjoying their romantic dinner. I wonder why they celebrate the gruesome end of a martyr, a saint in love. It is just another case of how people always thrive on the misery of others.

He said, "You must possess an inhuman bravery and determination to believe that humans are fundamentally good at heart." The damn bastard has some wisdom to spare when the amphetamine occasionally releases his brain from its fatal claws. Ironically, in his version of divine comedy, the amphetamine never let me go. I swallow his words, thinking they are universal truth. He was once my faith. An idol only my hands can reach. The sweet delusion of an addict's drug ballad. No one ever teaches me how the faithless will act when they betray their God. I hear someone say Judas wasn't a traitor by choice, he acted on the holy guidance. And Caesar's murder must happen for history's wheel to move forward. What about my religion?

I blow rings of smoke to the wind. On nights like this, I can always taste the saccharine flavor of his name on my tongue. He says it is the right thing to do. What he means is it's alright to sin. He says people can kill for worse. What he means is he holds no responsibility over the life he left behind. A field of corpses covered in white powder and the liquid dream.

No one was enough for Bambi. Perhaps I will be in this finale. When the curtain draws, the grandiose scheme ends, and I will be the last one standing, waiting for his ovation. I bite my nails; my teeth start chattering. I'm speeding toward my limit, and my mind is screaming defeat. Just a little more and this will be all behind. The nightmare barely begins pulling its shroud. I hit the brake. The tires screech on the unmarked road.

The lake is calm and peaceful, holding inside its bosom a thousand secrets deep. Slamming the door, I jog to the back of the car and open the trunk, my whole body becomes giddy. Every movement causes me to choke on air. In the total silent darkness of the winter night, I kick at the jammed car trunk, cursing my fate, nearly doubling myself over from the exhaustion of the whole ordeal. The thought of someone seeing me here drives my paranoic nightmare skyrocket and I consider driving the car down the lake.

From the trunk, the pungent smell of decaying flesh pervades my nose. I cry, helpless and cold in the newfound solitude. The help won't come. The salvation is not needed. I sink to the abyss, take a deep breath, and with another kick, push the trunk open with my sheer willpower, fervently praying that God is real. The black plastic bag lays neatly inside the closed space.

I heave it out, drag it to the edge of the freezing water, and sit down beside it. In the slight crack of the black plastic, his face is drowning in the gentleness of the eternal sleep. I stroke the handsome feature, the long eyelashes, the still soft lips, growing cold with death, the pair of dark brown eyes that cut me into tiny pieces of meat, now lays hidden behind the thin lids. He is nothing but a child, and I can save him. I really can. Where did I fail? I open the crack wider, revealing the pale skin and the hollow cheeks. Peace has found him, but the world has abandoned me.

Markus asked, "Where's Bambi?" Well, here he is. Dead.

I snuggle into the crook of his long neck that is bruised with the thick line of rope and inhale the sharp scent of sandalwood. The smell of decay is overpowering his warm, comforting perfume, but it doesn't matter. Memory is always stronger than what reality can bring. Placing a soft kiss on his forehead, his nose, then his frozen lips, I wonder about forgiveness. He said he wouldn't consider it a good thing. "Angela, baby, you must kill yourself along with your enemy when you decide to forgive them," Bambi smiled, his eyes glazed over.

I never knew what he saw in those off the floor moments. He was somewhere else – the past, the future, the could-be and the never, the whatever as long as it wasn't real. He forgot the fact that no matter how much he loved those illusions, the fever dreams won't love him back. "Angela, why are you named Angela?" Bambi toyed with my hair as he laughed at nothing at all. "There's no angel on Earth. You weren't meant to be here, my sweet Angela." And he was right. He was so Goddamn right. Sometimes, it takes a whole life of mistakes and regrets to know that things are simply never meant to be. My lips remain on his, sealing the fate I choose. The tears keep flowing for the life I gave away. Holding his stone-cold face in my heating palms, I whisper the final goodbye, knowing it is too late because I'm too far down the road and the way back has long vanished:

"Raymond, this is the first time and the last time I call you by that name. You spend your life rejecting that name, and I don't want to disappoint you, so I dare not mutter it in your presence. It's funny what fear will do to you, because I love it. Bambi or Raymond, they are both you. The famous rapper, the rockstar, or the discreet lover in the night – I love them all. I love you when you are on stage, performing your songs with the band. Standing in the spotlight, your sweat glistens and I never see anything shine so bright. You were born to be a star. No one can convince me otherwise. My brain is addled with the singular thought: I adore you. But to you, I was probably just another speck of dust among the heaps of body piling in front of you. You have the right to choose, after all. Fame. Power. Money. Why, Bambi Raymond, you have it all. So it keeps bugging me, Bambi, why did you choose me? Why must you bestow the sweet gift of your torturous love on me? Is it fun, watching me dancing as I burn myself in the flame of your creation?"

HE FALLS FIRST. SHE IS DESTROYED BY CHOICE.

I choke. My nose is bleeding. The red spatter of blood smears his otherwise paling, perfect face. For a moment of quiet revelation, I am mesmerized by the beauty of his death. Out of reach. Even in the moment when all is considered equal, he finds a way to be more equal than the rest.

"Hey, Raymond, tell me, do you still feel that threatful, suffocating solitude after death?" I snickered, remembering the first time I laid my eyes on this sweet of sin.

It was four years ago, in that crowded bar, Rendezvous. The noise almost gave me a seizure. The pungent smell of sweat and cheap perfume filled my nostril and reminded me how ugly and grotesque human existence was. I held onto Cecil's shoulders, barely able to keep myself from throwing up the manufactured orange juice I swallowed to stay afloat. Cecil, still alive then, was a good student at an art college uptown. She had this special talent for turning the swamp of this mess into something beautiful enough to make strangers cry. But being that good at drawing wasn't enough to save her from the comfort dreams in the embrace of the White Fairy – cocaine and amphetamine overdose.

I didn't see her bleak future then. I was too busy hanging on her thin arm for dear life, wondering for the thousandth time that night why I decided to come to this place. I was in my gap year, busy preparing for my university application. The future was so bright I had no other option but to be blinded by everything. Raymond entered the scene when I finally let go of the hold on my stomach and vomited all over his leather jacket and the expensive designer baggy pants.

"Oh hey, look who's coming to meet me tonight?"

His voice was sweet like the most potent honey I could buy in those flashy, upscale supermarkets – those glistening places where I never thought to enter. Not mine to hold. All mine to lose. He smiled at me, catching my drooping body in his strong arms. As his minty breath fanned over my overheated face, I kept thinking, 'This is it.' The platinum silver hair, slicked back to perfection. The cigarette hung loosely at his lips. The lopsided grin when he squinted his sparkling eyes, unfathomably dark, as he asked me in that same hoarse voice and low baritone: "What's your name, cutie pie?"

"Angela." I spoke without realizing my own voice in the trembling noise of the bar. There was no Cecil. No crowd. No cigarette smoke and cheap perfume smell. The world came back to life with just the two of us.

"So, Angel?" He smirked. I thought he found the name funny. It wasn't that.

"Yes."

"You look a bit uncomfortable here, Angel." He drew another smoke and flicked off the ash, gestured to the door. "Might coming outside a bit with me? For some air, you know."

"I don't. I mean, that's what I was thinking of doing, you know, before," I pointed vaguely toward the dance floor, where I was sure not the place he came from, "before you come."

"Really?" He cocked his eyebrow, seemingly saw through the lie I told, and many lies afterward. "Good. Big ideas often find a way to each other. Let's go, then?" He jerked his head toward the exit.

And I ignored Cecil's protest, his friends' groan, the guards in dark clothes surrounding him as he walked casually out of the bar with me in tow. Someone shouted out, "Bambi, you fucker, don't steal my girl." And he put up his middle finger with a mocking tease, "Too bad. Go fuck yourself, Markus."

The bar door closed behind us, barring the path to my future.

HE FALLS FIRST. SHE IS DESTROYED BY CHOICE.

Turning my head away from Cecil's tortured expression, I had a dark premonition that it was my first step on the ladder descending into madness. But madness wasn't the only thing Bambi Raymond would bring. Madness was his middle name.

To think that I loved him that much, and I love him still. What has become of the woman in me? She was destroyed. Not because she had no options. She chose her ending, didn't she? So many escape routes, and I settle for the simplest way to be free. LSD overdosed. An obvious ending to all drug junkies, especially someone who has plenty of dough to spend on those deathly, delicious stuff like Bambi. I stay out long enough, hang around places, show my face. My alibi should be strong. Biting my lips, I think about the last goodbye, hoping no one smells the decaying flesh in the back of my trunk as I drive down the road, speeding through the city night.

"It's okay, Raymond. You won't feel the pain of living anymore."

Tying the heavy bags of rocks to his cold feet, I push the corpse down the bank and watch it sink down the dark, autumn lake, dragging with it the human in me. The weeping willows shift their branches in the night air. An ending so befitting to the Emperor of Madness. Hamlet. Too bad, I wasn't good enough to be his Ophelia.

The surface of the water ripples for a while, calculating the weight it must take into its bosom. After a long, arduous moment, the lake goes back to its indifferent calmness. An unsettled peace on a stormy night. I light a cigarette, draw in a smoke, throw it down the lake, and walk away. Farewell, my only reason for living.

For now, I have another reason: Revenge.

The corpse smirks in the dark, watching me drive away on

the dimly lit road, saying, "Angela, if you want revenge, you must prepare two graves: one for me, one for your own."

About the Author

Thanh Dinh is a poet and storyteller whose work grapples with the intersection of loss, survival, and fragile hope. She was a finalist for the DVAN Fiction Contest and has been published in Wishbone Words, Story Quilt, and The Archipelago Magazine. On the best days, you can find her at the local library devouring the next best book on history. On the worst days, she writes like there's no tomorrow. Her work draws inspiration from Charles Bukowski, Sylvia Plath, Emily Dickinson, and the age-old traditions of Vietnamese storytelling, blending the mythic and the immediate with fearless intimacy.

You can connect with me on:
f https://www.facebook.com/writerly.books

Subscribe to my newsletter:
✉ https://forms.gle/ybPrVYFtUtJbBp3U7

Also by Thanh Dinh

Kill My Darling
A haunting, lyrical, and unflinching dive into the poisonous tangle of love, revenge, and addiction. When Angela's lover – famed rapper Bambi Raymond – spirals into a self-destructive abyss, Angela is pulled into a harrowing descent that ends in murder. Told in alternating timelines, the novel explores the complexities of their relationship, exposing the raw wounds of addiction, manipulation, and the corrosive hunger for justice. *Kill My Darling* is a dark, poetic testament to the brutal things we do for love, and the lies we tell ourselves to survive.

Chronicle of A Love Foretold

Chronicle of a Love Foretold is a lyrical, emotionally charged queer coming-of-age novel about Dong, a Vietnamese Canadian teenager trapped between filial duty and forbidden desire. When he learns his childhood best friend—and first love—Simon will be at a private school party, Dong risks everything to see him again, setting off a tender, secretive, and ultimately devastating reunion. Told through shifting timelines, poetic letters, and a heart laid bare, this novel explores the cost of freedom, the violence of love under surveillance, and what happens when the son a mother raised to be perfect finally chooses to live for himself. Gritty yet tender, aching with diasporic longing and queer first love, this is a story for anyone who's ever had to lie to survive, and dream to stay alive.

www.ingramcontent.com/pod-product-compliance
Lightning Source LLC
Chambersburg PA
CBHW032013030526
44119CB00063B/565